SO BLOW THE WINDS

SO BLOW THE WINDS
A Few Late Words

Keith Stanley-Mallett

With a last few verses by his wife, Elizabeth

ARTHUR H. STOCKWELL LTD
Torrs Park, Ilfracombe, Devon, EX34 8BA
Established 1898
www.ahstockwell.co.uk

© Keith & Elizabeth Stanley-Mallett, 2019
First published in Great Britain, 2019

The moral rights of the author have been asserted.

All rights reserved.
No part of this publication may be reproduced
or transmitted in any form or by any means,
electronic or mechanical, including photocopy,
recording, or any information storage and
retrieval system, without permission
in writing from the copyright holder.

British Library Cataloguing-in-Publication Data.
A catalogue record for this book is available
from the British Library.

ISBN 978-0-7223-4930-4 Paperback edition.
ISBN 978-0-7223-4931-1 Cloth-bound edition.
Printed in Great Britain by
Arthur H. Stockwell Ltd
Torrs Park   Ilfracombe
Devon EX34 8BA

DEDICATION

I dedicate this book to my wife, Elizabeth,
whose spirit passed on over Christmas 2018.
And who's sorely missed.

Previously published poems by the same author:
Little Traveller – Pumpkin Publications
Conspiracy of Faculties – Poetry Now, Forward Press, 1994
Yielding Forms – Poetry Now, 1994
One, That are We – Poetry Now, 1994
Two Minutes of Silence – Anchor Books, 1994
A Norfolk Winter Sunset – Poets England Series, Brentham Press, 1994
Come Silently to Me – Poetry Now, 1995
To the Eye – Poetry Now, 1995
World Wide Conceded Nationally – Poetry Now, 1996
Three Times Twenty – Poetry Now, 1996
I Believe in Betjeman – Poetry Now, 1996
Emotive Machine – Poetry Now, 1996
Essence of Time – Poetry Now, 1996
Poetic Visions – Poetry Now, 1996
Once Upon a Time – Poetry Now, 1996
The Red Fox – Anchor Books, 1997
Soul Winds – Poetry Now, 1997
Across a Timeless Threshold – Anchor Books, 1999
Mrs Batholomew's Door – Anchor Books, 1999
Electronic Life – United Press, 1999
Under An Indigo Moon – Arthur H. Stockwell Ltd, 2009
Beneath Rose-Lemon Skies – Arthur H. Stockwell Ltd, 2009
Before the Rainbow Fades – Arthur H. Stockwell Ltd, 2010
Between Night and Dancing Light – Arthur H. Stockwell Ltd, 2010
Beyond the Last Horizon – Arthur H. Stockwell Ltd, 2010
Upon a Past and Future Path – Arthur H. Stockwell Ltd, 2011
Odd Wit and Other Bits – Arthur H. Stockwell Ltd, 2011
Gilded Images – Arthur H. Stockwell Ltd, 2012
Flies Now The Spirit – Arthur H. Stockwell Ltd, 2013
Moments – Arthur H. Stockwell Ltd, 2015

FOREWORD

Last of the Last

Several times I've written,
the 'last book that is'.
But the spirit to write
would not agree.
So please believe, this really is the last
Book of contemporary verse that I shall write.

I do hope it is accepted in the spirit it is written.

Keith Stanley-Mallett

ACKNOWLEDGEMENTS

My grateful appreciation to my wife,
Elizabeth, for her help in producing this final work.

Also my special thanks to
Arthur H. Stockwell Ltd, publisher.

Part I

Collated Verse

By

Keith Stanley-Mallett

CONTENTS

The Magic of Spring	15
Serenity	16
The Village Bus	17
Spring Winds	18
Time's Years	19
Princely Love	20
Moon to Earth	21
Age	22
Aggression	23
Whither Wilt Thou?	24
Before, Now and After	25
Precipitation	26
Morning Mist	27
Flaming June	28
Wild Rose	29
Summertime	30
Butterfly	31
Realization	32
Green	33
Night	34
Love	35
Changes	36
The Watchers	37
Food	38
A View	39
Parliament, June 2018	40
Where?	41
Suddenly	42
Ghosts	43
Past Times	44
Conviction	45
In Sunshine and Shadow	46
Thoughts of the Author	47
So Blow the Winds	48
Life Changes	49
Profiteers	50

The Magic of Spring

When spring comes round
    With nature renewed,
Air, sweetly scented,
    Colours bright, imbued.

The skeletal trees
    Once more are re-robed
In bright woodland green
    Where blossoms fair, showed.

A warm breeze-like breath
    Touches all in its path,
Flowers nod at its touch
    As clouds drift on past.

Fields full of growth,
    Wildlife abounding,
Full of the energy
    Springtime, resounding.

Serenity

The serenity of the land
    Of England's lands and hills,
Her woodlands, fields and streams,
    Quaint villages, quiet wealds.

Green forests and farmlands,
    Old villages, church, on high,
Local shops, aging inns
    Set the scene of country life.

The sky above, a pale blue
    With soft white puffs of cloud,
Summertime warmth pervades all
    Whilst cattle to rest, lie down.

Hum of insects fills the air,
    Butterflies flit bloom to bloom,
On England's lands and hills
    Serenity, sweet in June.

The Village Bus

The country village bus
    Comes each day at ten o'clock,
To take folk to market
    And the town's local shops.

Calling at each village
    For those who need to shop,
Down the lane it motors
    'Midst farmers' gazing stock.

A lifeline to the folk
    The country village bus,
It takes them here and there
    In a way that they trust.

The bus returns them home
    Around mid afternoon,
Stopping at each village,
    It really is, a boon.

Spring Winds

'Tis near the month of June
    Approaching summertime,
Yet the weather stays cold
    When by now, should be fine.

Each day we look to see
    If the sun is shining,
Still the weather is cold
    Wind, cloud, combining.

It really is too bad
    We need the sun to shine,
To rid us of winter
    Warming the land sublime.

So blows the chilly winds
    Nigh unto summertime,
'Tis old England's weather
    As people know and sigh.

Time's Years

The passing years slide by
>Mostly unremembered,
Uncounted or numbered
>The mind not encumbered.

Until the time arrives
>When at an age mature,
Your mind begins to search
>For memories unclear.

To find your living past
>Actions and deeds pursued,
Thus, of physical strength
>Or of knowledge ensued.

Yet on deep reflection
>Reaching now, old age,
Truth only, does remain
>For the mind to engage.

Therefore rest the mind,
>Consider life to come,
Will it be unknowing?
>Will awareness be won?

Princely Love

'Twas a moment serene
    'Midst cameras and press,
When the young royal prince
    Married his sweet duchess.

In the chapel royal
    The music rose on high,
Trumpets loudly sounded
    As the couple pass'd by.

Standing now, side by side
    They spoke their vows in truth,
As each to each did give
    A ring of loving proof.

The royal carriage waits,
    Music and trumpets sound,
Onward to Frogmore House
    Horses and couple bound.

Mounted troops from Horse Guards,
    Blues and Royals, splendid,
Crisp sound of marching feet
    Full wrought as intended.

Good luck and a good life
    To Henry and Rachael,
As Duke and as Duchess
    True part of this nation.

Moon to Earth

Seven days to a week,
    Thirty days each month's run,
Three hundred 'n' sixty-five
    Revolving round the sun.

For millions of years
    The earth traversed its course,
Turning in its orbit
    Around the life-born source.

Companion to the earth
    The moon does orbit close,
Illuminating night
    Like a high-flying ghost.

Each day, each month, each year
    Wound up like clockwork toys,
The earth circles the sun
    As moon to earth employs.

Age

Age is ever present
    No matter who you are,
Certainly not, your age
    Or whether near or far.

For age is just a word
    Recalling those past times,
On how old one can be
    Determined by the signs.

Of an age 'n' ages old
    Ancient days long ago,
A term for past-gone years
    Thus, to confirm it's so.

Age means growing older
    As determined each year,
Whether still young or old
    Time is always revered.

Aggression

Tell me, then, why is it
    That men are persuasive?
Why one man causes hell!
    Becoming aggressive.

There is no gain in war
    Nothing is ever won!
Pain and destruction
    Only this, by the gun.

No matter the machine
    By land, sea, or by air,
Each battle causes loss
    Of those who courage share.

Aggression never pays
    It is a well-known fact,
One must fight aggression
    With wisdom and with tact.

Wherever it is found,
    This age-old human fault,
Must be swiftly conquered,
    Or the future means nought.

Whither Wilt Thou?

A saying from the past,
> Whither wilt thou wander?
Across the old wild lands
> To distant parts, yonder?

Thus, places far away
> Over land, sea and more,
For the adventurous
> Who reach a foreign shore.

Or marvel at the earth
> The beauty of nature,
Developing ideas
> Creating the future.

Yet, just to sit and muse,
> Wondering thus sublime,
Thinking of this and that
> Ideas and thoughts to find.

For such is a poet
> Seeking thus, for longer,
Finding life's hidden truths
> For that mind to ponder.

Before, Now and After

When you dig unturned earth
    Or split the weathered rock,
Holding time's old secrets
    Held still, as under lock.

For part now of our earth
    Are prehistoric bones,
From early days of time
    Now turned to cold stone.

The monsters and the small
    Who trod with heavy step,
Or fled on tiny feet
    Away to safety set.

Remote now are those times
    Into distance faded,
'Tis we who now do stand
    Like them, alone, unaided.

No matter who or where,
    For time has no master,
Life evolves and changes
    Before, now and after.

Precipitation

'Tis the rising moisture
    Lifting high from the lands
Causing clouds to gather
    In black foreboding bands.

Until, with moisture swell'd
    Precipitates withal,
Thus the clouds release
    Their needed waterfall.

For water is to life
    As the air is to breathe,
One without the other
    Would leave us deep in need.

From the sea to the sky
    From the sky to the land,
Precipitation gives
    Life to nature and man.

Morning Mist

$\mathcal{L}$ike the rising of ghosts
    From the wet morning ground,
The early springtime mists
    Gather without a sound.

Mysterious vapour
    Forming, clinging and damp,
Obscuring sight and sound
    Like shades around a lamp.

Arising from the ground
    The morning mist clings low,
A mysterious cloak
    Hiding all things below.

The laying mist endures
    Until the rising sun,
Which slowly dissipates
    The morning veil, low-hung.

So daylight advances
    On Mercury's fast wing,
Dissipating the mist
    As the birds begin to sing.

Flaming June

So arrives June the first
    The first day of summer.
Will the sun brightly shine,
    Warming us, like Mother?

Or will the skies remain
    Overcast and dreary?
'Tis likely it will rain
    Making us more weary.

For such is old England
    Her place upon the earth,
Whereby she is showered
    To freshly keep her worth.

Although it would be nice
    To see a bit more sun,
Water is essential
    For life and ev'ry one.

Wild Rose

Out in the countryside
    Or in vast empty lands,
It is most surprising
    To find a plant that stands –

Proud, tall and colourful,
    Delicate of flower,
In nature's own fair shade
    Like an elfin bower.

Petal, pale pink of hue
    Honey yellow at heart,
Life's natural colours
    Full fairy-soft in part.

Self-sown by ancient winds
    In byways stand supreme,
The wild, wild English rose
    A land and hedgerow queen.

Summertime

Once more 'tis summertime
    The days are warm and bright,
Birdsong rich and varied
    Fills the air, morn 'til night.

Roses in bright full bloom
    Colourfully adorn
Both hedgerow and garden,
    In their scented bright form.

The buzzing insects fly
    Amidst the garden green,
Busy bees inspecting
    Each open flower seen.

Butterflies erratic
    Fly to each coloured bloom,
Whilst busy hedge sparrows
    Flit and hop, for 'tis June.

Butterfly

Butterfly, butterfly
    Quickly you flutter by,
Butterfly, butterfly
    So swiftly, darting fly.

From flower to flower
    For nectar-like honey,
Quick hither and thither
    Whilst day is full sunny.

So delicate a form
    Fluttering, silently,
Your beauty and colour
    Formed beguilingly.

In the countryside fair
    Or in parklands so green,
With beds full of fresh blooms
    Are the butterflies seen.

From upland to valley
    In each garden they pry,
These bright-coloured insects
    Are a joy to the eye.

Realization

The years pass quickly by
    Unnoticed as a rule,
For you are too busy
    To notice this old truth.

Yet slowly you begin
    To understand the fact,
You are getting older
    Perhaps, on the last track.

Thus, old time speeds on by
    Advancing the faster,
Uncounted are the years
    Becoming the master.

'Til realization
    Finally hammers home,
Your days are nearly done
    Will you have to atone?

For unbeknown to some,
    There is a future world,
Beyond that known to us,
    In which the spirit dwells.

Green

Grey-green and rich red-green
    Bright yellow-green 'n' blue,
So many shades of green
    All leaves of nature true.

Some of grey and silver,
    Gold and purple also,
All bright and colourful
    The brighter the more so.

Great woodlands and forests
    Have their share of colour,
Parkland, weald and upland
    With many another.

For grass also is green
    As red, yellow, white 'n' blue
Are the hues of flowers,
    Nature's family, true.

Night

Night is mysterious
    With its creeping shadows,
Strong unearthly noises
    Like ghosts on All Hallows.

Trees rustle and whisper
    In the soft gentle breeze,
Whilst a hidden owl calls
    From amidst darken'd trees.

Above, the night-filled sky
    Reveals a pale-lit moon,
Which hides behind the clouds
    Casting an eerie gloom.

A roaming fox calls out
    Distant, melancholy,
As erratic bats fly
    In the dark air oddly.

A gust of wind quickly
    Stirs the darken'd night
Reminding us that life
    Can cause delight or frights.

Love

Let your heart play host to love,
>Your mind discern true feeling,
As your soul acquires new depths
>Embracing love's meaning.

For love can be elusive
>Although the heart may flutter,
Discern your feelings true
>Ere, love's words, you utter?

Thus, false love has no magic
>No depth of feeling that grew,
Be wise and take your time
>To understand anew.

You will know the one to be
>When you find the love that's true,
Your heart will burst for joy
>As love embraces you.

Changes

'Tis summer so it's said
    Over western countries,
Now is the month of June
    Yet shows not the bound'ries.

'Twixt spring and the autumn
    Weather appears the same,
Just wet, cold, wind and dull
    Regardless, the month's name.

Where have our summers gone?
    It all appears the same,
Soon old winter will join
    Those months of summer's name.

Spring and winter shall be
    Our new climate and fate,
With summer and autumn
    The new lengthened state.

Now, what once were seasons
    Have changed and gone by,
Time has wrought the changes
    Thus, only time knows why –

NOW TIME HAS SHOWN!

The Watchers

We are quickly coming
    To that point in earth time,
When the truth will be known
    About those age-old signs.

At last the time is close
    For a true first meeting,
With those whom space do fly
    Now, for contacts seeking.

Throughout all history
    Those first yet unknown craft,
Are seen around the world
    Whilst in mystery cast.

Yet time fast approaches
    For this meeting of minds,
A few have met before
    In better times, we find.

Old time has passed by
    A new time now begins,
Soon will be this meeting
    'Twixt earth and godlike beings.

Food

𝆑ast food, slow food, weak food,
    With many others too,
In their entirety
    Awaiting for you.

Tough food, soft food and rich,
    There's such variety,
Just choose your food with care
    As you like it to be.

Select your food wisely
    Though some may not agree;
We can't all eat the same
    So must choose precisely.

So what we like we eat
    We are all different,
We are thus full lucky
    To be so well content.

Food is what you make it
    So try to choose the best,
It's in your interest
    To eat your meals with zest.

A View

I sit by a window
    That overlooks a field,
Bathed in golden light
    A shining sun, revealed.

The trees beyond the field
    Are home to large black crows,
Who chat both morn and eve
    Just arguing in rows.

Wild rabbits run and play
Amongst the flowering shrubs,
As the warmth of the day
    States summer, which they love.

Insects and butterflies
    Both fly from here to there,
Whilst dogs lazily sleep
    In the dry cosy air.

So, as I sit this day
    Looking upon summer,
I try to understand
    Why others, like thunder!

Parliament, June 2018

How much are politics
    Akin to the saying
Of 'jolly hockey sticks',
    By Members a-failing?

To understand in depth
    What really should be done,
Just shrug the motion off
    Move on to the next one.

Prime Minister's Questions
    Ev'ry Wednesday shows,
Too much hilarity
    Will see base remarks grow.

'Tis more like a classroom
    Full of cheeky children,
Emotions can be strong
    Like winds in the wild fen.

They need to knuckle down
    Pull together as one.
Stop the silly nitpicks
    Then battles can be won.

Where?

Just where do we belong?
    We've been so long alone,
Most believe that the earth
    Is our true ancient home.

There is a new power
    Within the minds of some,
An understanding spark
    That others here, have come.

Many long ages past
    Before man trod the earth,
Others with knowledge came
    To mine and build at first.

Then did create at last
    A thinking humanoid
To help them in their work,
    Thus appeared girl and boy.

Adam and Eve by name
    Began humanity,
As father and mother
    To human totality.

Thus, part of this planet
    Yet part of the stars,
A far distance they came
    To earth, and to Mars.

Suddenly

'Tis summer, so it's said
    As the wind bends the trees
Below a darken'd sky,
    Buffeting the green leaves.

The birds erratic fly
    Against the sudden blast,
Whilst the shroud-blackened clouds
    Like unto night are cast.

A jagged flash of light
    Brightens the heavens above,
Whilst a bark of thunder
    Sounds menacing enough.

Then suddenly the storm
    Just quickly fades away,
As summer storms just do
    Freshening the air today.

For summer's heat and dust
    Builds up to quickly lay,
Thus these short lasting storms
    Clean air and earth this way.

Ghosts

The term 'ghostly image'
    Can be attributed
To various spirits,
    Seen, and unseen, muted.

Some are between, silent,
    Trapp'd in the netherworld,
Yet also caught in time,
    Thus to exist, compelled.

Whilst many after death
    Hold tight the bonds of earth,
Impelled by strong feelings
    That, of personal worth.

There are ghosts in torment
    Who moan and are bad-tempered,
Looking for an answer
    To something remembered.

Others become nasty,
    They terrify people,
Thus should be made to go
    Where they can rid evil.

Past Times

The old clock still stands, where
    It has stood many years,
Striking the passing hours
    Of each day's news and fears.

Many long years have passed
    Since it was first brought here,
To stand so regally
    In the hall, so revered.

Now, an age has passed
    Together with the folk,
One or two remember
    Times that are now remote.

Old faces long since gone,
    Children grown and married,
Changes to the old house,
    Times appear more hurried.

Still the old clock stands, where
    It was placed so long ago,
Ticking the years away
    To time's true constant flow.

Conviction

Are the people of earth
> So ignorant of time?
For history has shown
> Their failure to define –

The ignorance of man
> Over history's past,
Humanity has prov'd
> They must master the task –

Of living together
> On this fine planet,
To outlaw bloody war
> Find a way to ban it.

Once mankind understands
> That war not only kills,
It holds progression back
> As anger and hate, builds.

Humans must come to terms
> Overcome suspicions,
Their minds must think as one,
> Now speak with conviction!

In Sunshine and Shadow

We have to carry on
    To face whatever ills,
Whether it's in sunshine
    Or dark'd shadows fill.

The human race abides
    By what it thinks is best,
Does not know the answer
    To many evil quests.

Humanity depends
    On what is right in life,
There is only one right:
    Freedom to see the light.

Whoever tries to block
    Humanity's true path,
Will fail in their efforts
    As they have in the past.

Many times have dark minds
    Tried to change history.
In sunshine and shadow
    Sunshine has victory.

Thoughts of the Author

When you are elderly
    Have lived many years,
Life loses its sparkle
    Yet gains so many fears.

You have lived the long years
    Seen life of diverse kinds,
Have done so many things
    In a busy lifetime.

Those times have now gone by
    I stand a pensioner,
Writing poetic works
    Whilst able to confer.

I write and always have
    For the pleasure of words,
Words that create pictures
    Which in the mind transfers –

The poet's written word
    To pictures of the kind,
Which I, do wish will stay
    Within the reader's mind.

So Blow the Winds

So blow the winds at times
    From gentle soft breezes,
To raging wintry gales
    So cold, water freezes.

From springtime to summer
    You get a lighter wind,
That gently moves the leaves
    Light of touch, near-elfin.

Yet comes the rising storm,
    The harsh downpour of rain,
Damaging bloom and plant
    'Til the sun shines again.

Autumn winds when they come
    Remove warmth of summer,
Cooling the still warm air
    Like an absent lover.

Thus to snowy winter
    Temperature ice-cold,
'Tis the year's sunless time
    Brightened by Christmas bold.

Yet, the winds blow worldly
    Across the planet's face,
For politics and war
    Are the winds of our race!

Life Changes

So the weeks, months and years
    Continue, part of time,
As they have always done
    Under moon and sunshine.

From ancient days long past
    Prehistoric ages,
Life has grown and changed
    Develop'd in stages.

We, are the descendants
    Of the first humans wrought,
Now we live in cities,
    Further, to stars have sought.

Time appears so lengthy
    Back through periods gone,
Yet, 'tis the future's path
    Life changes weak and strong.

So the centuries run
    Continuing new life,
Progressively learning
    How to live without strife.

Profiteers

We will give you a loan
    If you're short of money,
Since you are now alone
    The days are not sunny.

Those bright times now are gone
    Life has become tiresome,
To live without money
    Can become most fearsome.

'Tis not always the fault
    Of those without the means,
Just the way of business
    Profiting not, it seems.

Those with the means care not
    As those without money,
Yet cause more hurt in life
    Adding to the worry.

Money must be earned
    Yet, if there is no way,
How can those without it
    Live now, from day to day?

Part II

Verses to End With

By

Elizabeth Stanley-Mallett

A few latecomers from me finalize this last book.

We do hope you find our work interesting.

Elizabeth

CONTENTS

Love's Tribute	57
Life	58
Summer Solstice	59
Four	60
Loneliness	61
Where the Bluebells Bloom	62

Love's Tribute

It's that time of year again
    And I must put pen to paper,
Saying how much I love you
    Rather now than later.

I quite often fail to please
    Cannot get things right,
The computer goes and crashes
    Blanking everything in sight.

You take great care of me
    I am a burden in your life,
I know I am very lucky,
    Privileged to be your wife.

Over the years we've had fun
    Where humour has a poke,
Collecting so many puns
    Making our own pack of jokes.

So, with love I pen these words
    My clumsy kind of verse,
Lovingly we'll stumble on
    For better, or for worse.

Life

Life is simply a journey
    From the moment we are born,
Adventures and exploring
    Bringing accolades or scorn.

The joy seeing your children
    Grow, marry and settle down,
You hope they have true values
    And do not behave like clowns.

To find our source of origin
    Our pilgrimage needs to soar,
Where lies the master plan at
    The universe central core.

A vastly different realm
    Full of lively joy and fun,
Paradise to be enjoyed
    Chances there for everyone.

Summer Solstice

The longest day in the year
    When hot summer, supreme reigns,
Long and sultry humid days
    Warm nights where sleep is in vain.

Relics of the old Druids
    Who were soundly thrash'd, by Rome,
Banished to Anglesey
    Nowhere like their proper home.

Taking place on a green plain
    At the monument Stonehenge,
The worshippers of sunrise
    Chanted their age-old refrain.

'Tis a time of enchantment
    Magic is felt in the air,
Vibrations will travel far
    From ancient circles there.

Four

The bringer of good fortune
    'Tis said of the four-leaved clover,
Many of us need the luck
    Before our life is over.

The mother with four sons
    One now far adrift,
Disowned without a reason
    In spite of special gifts.

Gospels first in New Testament –
    Matthew, Mark, Luke, John –
Relating as best they could
    Christ really had not gone.

Four points of the compass
    North, south east and west,
Blowing four winds around the world
    Forever, without rest.

Four seasons of the year –
    Winter, spring, summer, fall –
Our form now is blessed, for
    From the slime we did crawl.

To foretell a mystic gift used by
    Romanies of olden days,
Casting by a crystal ball
    Forbidden but it pays.

Four letters in 'love'
    My feelings for you,
Deep and eternal
    My love ever true.

Loneliness

Living by oneself when old
    Is not so very funny,
Just to see a friendly face
    Better than finding money.

Footsteps coming up the path
    Is it the usual mail?
Dropped through the letter box
    Without the usual hail.

Yearning for telephone calls
    From a family member,
Who was the recent caller?
    Too distant to remember.

Thinking back to wartime days
    When we were all together,
Seeing each other day t' day
    In summer or cold weather.

It is hard to understand
    What it is to be lonely
Scared of unknown loud noises
    Targeted at me only.

Where the Bluebells Bloom

Under the lovely mountain ash tree
    A carpet of flowers blue,
Where you are laid to rest
    Side by side just me and you.

My spindle tree has berries red
    Adorning our verdant plot,
In this special cemetery
    We've tied our eternal knot.

The spirits of both of us
    Frequently visit home,
Where happy years we spent
    Together, not alone.

Joined in life in many ways
    Our final path is strewn,
Our essence, forever will stay with
    Bluebells in full bloom.